THE OCTOPUS CODE

'How to rise up from the depths of the Ocean of Life'

Dr Royston G. Lawrence

ISBN : 9798733960630
: Independently published

Cover design by: Heather Rice

CONTENTS

Acknowledgements

I have to thank a number of people for their help in producing this book. Firstly I would like to thank Heather Rice for her beautiful artwork, which is the front cover of this book and for proofreading it. I am also very grateful to Mel Eves for proofreading this book and for the constructive feedback he gave me on it.

Next, I would like to thank Des McCabe and Jimmy Ryan for running the 'WorkitOut' workshop program which gave me the inspiration and courage to complete this book. I would like to especially thank, the excellent 'E-book' support group run by Heather and Helen as part of the program which gave me the support and help when needed to finish this book.

I would also like to thank Chris Rushton, for a number of helpful discussions, about my ideas for the chapters, during the early stages of writing this book.

I also have to thank Mike, Jayney and all of the Creation crew not forgetting Jayne, who have taught so much me about personal development and self-belief.

I would also like to thank Danica, Sophie and Keith for giving me the initial inspiration to write a self-help book.

I would also like to thank Manth and Emma for inviting me to the Healing garden at Buddhafield for a number of years and for providing a safe space there, in which I could explore the ideas for this book.

I also have to thank my good friend White Hawk, for some helpful advice on writing style and for proofreading part of this book.

I would also like to thank my late Aunt, Jean Edwards, who did all she could to help me become a holistic therapist and believed I could do it, when no one else did.

Finally I would like to thank my late Mom, Dad and brother who helped me on my journey through life, and taught me much great wisdom.

Introduction

Are you drowning in the ocean of life, not sure how to achieve what you want in life? You may be lacking direction and be unsure what path you wish to take in life. That's okay most people don't realise that we live in the ocean of life, and it can be tough to navigate it, without help. This self-help book will help you navigate it, through new thinking, which I have outlined in 8 steps called the 'Octopus Code'. If you follow all these steps in sequence your new thinking, will empower you to achieve your life goals and allow you to rise up from the depths of the ocean of life.

CHAPTER 1- FINDING THE OCEAN FLOOR

Life on this planet should be exciting, rewarding, full of new challenges and make you thankful for every day you wake up because one day you will leave this planet behind and all you will have to look back on before you die will be your memories. What will those memories be of? Remember nobody on their deathbed ever said "I wished I had spent more time at work". We forget that we are all trading time on this planet to do work, but time is the most precious commodity we have in our lives and no matter how rich you are you can never buy back time. Nobody on this planet was born just to work to pay bills and die. I believe we all came to this planet with a purpose to achieve something. I am sure, you have life goals you want to achieve. I am also sure some people have laughed at you and mocked you mercilessly for having these goals that's okay I will explain how to deal with those kinds of people later.

I have titled this book 'The Octopus Code' because it uses eight self-help steps to put your life back on track, once you have learned them all you will be empowered to realise your unfulfilled life goals. The octopus' analogy is also useful in the type of changes you need to make, but I will explain more about that in later chapters.

The key analogy I am going to use in this book is that life is like the ocean, indeed I will refer to it is as the 'ocean of life' because of their synergy. Just like life, the ocean is a complex ecosystem, it has several layers, a rich diversity of species and it is beautiful, but it can also be very cruel. The layers of ocean are also dependent on each other for their survival just like in life.

The first step of the Octopus code is to find the ocean floor of your life. This is your own personal baseline the point at which you think I can't go on like this something has to change. This is an important place to define, as it is at that point you are most likely to begin to assess your life goals and how to achieve them.

The level of the of the ocean floor will be different for everybody, some people will find it easily, others will spend many years falling through the ocean of life before they ever reach it, and of course some people will never get there. The ocean floor will be at a different level for every person as what one person can tolerate another may not be able to process.

The ocean floor of life, at first glance may not seem like the best place to be, it can be dark and gloomy with not a lot of life on it, but the important point in finding it is you have hit the lowest ebb in your life. This is important because the only way you can go now is up, after all there is nothing lower than your ocean floor. Once you have found your ocean floor, use this affirmation daily until you start to feel better about your situation 'I have found my ocean floor now the only way is back up, I have taken the first step on the path to achieving my life goals'.

According to Tony Robbins 'Change happens when the pain of staying the same is greater than the pain of change' and that will only happen when you are on the ocean floor. Now that you are on the ocean floor this is a good time for reflection, firstly you need to identify how you got there. What happened in your life to bring you here? Was it a single event in your life or a series of events? Can you recognise a trigger or triggers which have brought you to where you are now? These are the important questions you need to ask yourself in order to understand how you got to your own personal ocean floor. Because if you don't understand how you fell to the ocean floor in the first place, how are you going to be able to get to the surface again? Doing this self-analysis will allow you to measure the depth of your problem. Whilst doing this analysis you can visualise your own personal emotional plumb line with a float at the end which symbolises your life goals, what you are doing is letting the plumb line out until the float is able sit upright freely in the water. This symbolises your life being back on track and being empowered to achieve your life goals. The amount of line you have to let out is the depth of your problem, you can imagine markers on the line which are milestones along the way to sorting out your problems. However, like a real plumb line you have to make sure it does not get snagged otherwise it won't give an accurate depth reading, in this case you don't want your emotional plumb line to get snagged on emotional rocks which could distort your depth reading. For example, if you have come to your ocean floor because of a bad life choice such as addiction, that's okay don't make the problem worse by beating yourself up about it emotionally. Addicts get clean every day the best thing you have done for yourself is admitting you have a problem; most people don't have the courage to do this. You may have had problems in the past that were not your fault, that's okay too, but what you do with the rest of your life is your fault. Another quote from Tony Robbins is useful to remember at this point 'Your past does not equal your future'.

Whilst doing this analysis it is also helpful to visualize yourself as a diver on the ocean floor inspecting your emotional plumb line, and although we don't want the plumb line to get snagged on the emotional rocks, it is important to acknowledge the presence of the rocks and how they make you feel. These feelings are important and you need to deal with them, but you have to accept they were associated with your past and no longer serve you. You have to accept you need to change and you can't let these feelings imprison you anymore. Otherwise, you can end up trapped at the bottom of the ocean of life, a bit like a lobster stuck in a lobster pot, fighting madly to get out but ultimately still trapped.

The next thing you have to do whilst on the ocean floor of life is to decide that from now on you are going to take back control of your life, and accept that everything that happens to you in your life is because of you and the choices you make. This can be a very difficult thing for a lot of people to accept as we are all used to blaming other people or things for our problems, such as the government, your partner, your job, your car or even where you live. A good ocean analogy is the puffer fish which when it gets scared sucks in water, so it expands and protrudes its spines so it is safe from attack. When you blame other people, or things, for your problems you are doing the same, you are just making the problems bigger and more spiky and thus difficult to address, you are becoming the puffer fish. What you need to do is emotionally deflate yourself and look at your problems objectively without emotion, try imagining you were advising someone else, and take the advice you would give them. I am sure you have given other people good advice on their problems, you just need to get better at facing and analysing your own problems.

Another issue you have to acknowledge and work through is there may be people in your life stuck on the emotional rocks. These people, using our ocean analogy, would be limpets, that is by fear or other emotion they are stuck to a particular situation or behaviour which they find difficult to escape from, but like limpets given the right conditions they are capable of locomotion and moving to a different, perhaps better, rock. Of course, some people on the emotional rocks may be more like barnacles, stuck permanently to a situation or a behaviour because they feed off it. You have to accept you are never going to change those type of people and move on in your life without them. Otherwise, you are just going to waste a lot of time trying to prise people who are barnacles off the emotional rocks and then getting mad and frustrated because you can't do it. It could even be that trying to do this is part of the reason that brought you to the ocean floor of life. If so, now is a good time to acknowledge this and move on.

Now unfortunately the ocean floor of life is not without it's dangerous visitors, whilst you are there you have to watch out for two types of people, the first type of people are those who are the sharks in our ocean analogy. People who have a shark personality are ruthless and reckless in getting what they want and have no qualms about using and abusing other people to do it. I am sure you have met many people in your life who have shark personalities and like real sharks they are not necessarily all bad, but, at the moment in your position on the ocean floor of life, you are probably feeling like a very small fish the ocean equivalent of whitebait, and thus are a very easy meal for a shark. Unless you want to get torn apart again and be thrown back on the ocean floor of life in an even worse state my advice is **avoid the sharks**. Now of course you could be a shark who has fallen to the ocean floor of life, perhaps you were too ruthless and reckless in trying to get what you wanted, and karma caught up with you, and you lost it all. That's okay no-one is here to judge you, you just have to recognise that it was your shark like behaviour that has led you to the ocean floor of life and if you want to progress off it again you have to alter your behaviour. The second type of danger on the ocean floor of life are the people who are whales in our ocean analogy. People who have whale personalities just reach out and suck everything in including you if you are not careful, mix it up a bit and just spit it out at random. Once again, I am sure you have met people who have dragged you into stuff you didn't want to get involved in, mixed you up a bit and then just discarded you when they were done. Again, people, with whale personalities are not all bad, and of course some people probably don't even realise that they have a whale personality. However, you have to remember you are here to deal with your own problems, and don't need to be sucked into somebody else's crazy messed up life with all its problems, you have enough to deal with yourself, so like the sharks my advice is **avoid the whales**.

Another peril to consider whilst on the ocean floor is money, now I am sure you have probably in the past thought that the answer to all your problems in life was to have more money. "If only I had more money my life would be so much better", you have probably thought. Unfortunately, it doesn't work like that, just having money doesn't bring true happiness, because money is a finite resource and when it runs out so does the happiness it brings. This is why a lot of lottery winners end up broke again because they don't understand this fact, they just keep spending hoping spending more money will bring them happiness, which of course it doesn't. What you really want in life is more time, perhaps for yourself, or your family so you can experience life, make some fantastic memories and find inner peace, you will then have a true lasting happiness which does not rely on money. If one of your life goals is to earn more money so you can spend more time with your family, there is nothing wrong with that. The problem comes when people indulge in the reckless pursuit of money above all else, they often develop a shark personality and if they are not careful sooner or later, they burn themselves out and end up on the ocean floor of life. Have you considered has your shark personality and love of money above all else brought you to the ocean floor of life? Again if it has that's okay, but you have to recognise that this is the problem that brought you here, or guess what, you are just going to do the same again. You need to develop a different relationship with money, to view it merely as an energy to be exchanged for goods and services, which was all it was ever intended to be. However, somehow money enslaved us and turned us into addicts who would do anything to possess it, and that is when our relationship with money became unhealthy. If you recognise yourself in any of the behaviours I have just described, then clearly changing your relationship with money is something you need to do before you can move off the ocean floor. Using our ocean analogy again you can view money as the equivalent of kelp forests, green, attractive and a valuable resource which can support a lot of fish, but swim too far into it and you can become ensnared in it and it can become choking. You need to become a more intelligent octopus who knows how far to swim into the forest, before it gets dangerous.

There are also a few of types of people who choose to remain on the ocean floor of life because that is where it suits them to be. Some people use the lure of a bright and wonderful future to suck in vulnerable people and take advantage of them, they would be the angler fish in our ocean analogy, not pretty but part of the ocean of life. These types of people stay at the bottom of the ocean of life because that is where their prey is and they have no interest in moving on. Some people are afraid of change and choose to remain stuck in their shells, at the first sign of trouble they just go into their shell and hide, at certain times in their lives they may move into a bigger more shinier shell but it is still a shell. These people would be the hermit crabs in our ocean analogy. There are also some people who choose to stay in a trench at the bottom of the ocean floor of life, because they have become literally entrenched in their behaviour over a long period of time. It is difficult to move them out of the trench into new situations because they tend to get scared, break away and return to the trench they know. Using our ocean analogy they would be starfish because of their ability to shed a limb when attacked and return to their trench. Again, you may recognise some people in your life with these personalities or even yourself amongst these people, the important point is to recognise this and to move on. If your desire is strong enough the majority of people can lift themselves off the ocean floor of life again.

In summary the first step in the Octopus code is to find your personal ocean floor, survey it and measure the distance emotionally back to the level you can begin to achieve your life goals. This will give you an idea of the depth of your problems and of the length of time your recovery will take, which will of course be different for everyone. You need to take some time for reflection whilst you are there and consider carefully how you got there, indeed you may need to stay there for a long time until you are sure you have a clear answer, but of course whilst you are there you have to watch out for the sharks, whales, and angler fish which are the hazards whilst there. You may also have to become a different type of person if you don't want to be stuck there permanently. Armed with a clear understanding of your problems you will be ready to start to move off the ocean floor and for the next step of the Octopus code.

CHAPTER 2 - DEALING WITH THE JELLYFISH

Now you have a clear understanding of your problems, the next thing to do is to come up with a small, simple, measurable step which you can take to begin to move off your personal ocean floor. It is very important that this step is measurable, otherwise you will take no action and you will remain on the ocean floor. For example, 'I want a different or better job' is no good as a step because it is not measurable and allows you to take no action. A better step is 'I will e-mail my C.V. to 100 companies and see if I can get a job interview', because at least you will get some responses and you may find you are not as unemployable as you thought, and that you can begin to move off the ocean floor.

The major problem you face in trying to formulate this step, is at the moment, you are feeling pretty low. Using my ocean analogy, you are probably feeling small and insignificant like whitebait a very tiny fish. Unfortunately, this makes you very easy prey for the people in life who are the ocean equivalent of jellyfish.

The fact that the jellyfish has survived 650 million years in the ocean without a brain is probably a great source of inspiration for many people. Unfortunately, it is precisely this type of brainless person who as soon you try to take your single step off the ocean floor will attack you. This attack will be along the lines of 'How can you do anything with your life, you are too stupid/ugly ever to do that". People who are jellyfish in the ocean of life have become conditioned by society to what they can achieve and will instinctively attack anyone who tries to do something different. They may even kid themselves them they are doing it to protect you because they don't want to see you fail. Unfortunately, we all live in a conformist society and we are all taught to behave in certain way from a young age, and until recently what you could achieve was limited by your social class. Thus, the fact that these people have a jellyfish personality is not entirely their fault, they have just been conditioned to be like that over a long time. They have probably failed at some stage in life having been forced to conform. However, they are deadly at this stage in your progress from the ocean floor, they are your quickest route back there, perhaps to stay there permanently. If you want to make progress on your journey from the ocean floor you need to deal with the jellyfish, so the second step of the octopus code is **deal with the jellyfish**.

The best way to deal with the jellyfish in your life is by undertaking personal development, you can do this by reading or listening to 20 minutes of a personal development book or audio a day. If you do 10 minutes in the morning and 10 minutes at night, most people can make room to do this in their life no matter how busy they are. There is of course a large amount of personal development material available these days, my advice would be to choose material by someone who resonates with you and your life story so far. That way you are more likely to continue with your personal development journey as at first it may well be quite difficult, but as Confucius says ' A journey of a thousand miles begins with a single step'. After a just a short period of doing self-development you may still be a small fish in the ocean but with the important difference you will now, in personal development, have an important ally which is the ocean equivalent of a leather-back turtle, and guess what leather back turtles eat jellyfish!

Doing personal development may seem weird at first but it is a key step in continuing your journey upwards and away from the ocean floor, done consistently you will develop such a positive mental attitude you will be impervious to attack by people with jellyfish personalities. This will then allow you to ride on the back of your new found turtle ally and let it take you to new heights in your life, some you may not have previously thought possible. As you move off the ocean floor of life you have to embrace change and be willing, if necessary, to move on and leave your old life, and maybe even some friends who no longer serve you, behind. They may be stuck on the emotional rocks I mentioned in the previous chapter. This may seem harsh and difficult to understand but to quote Jim Rohn 'You are the average of the 5 people you spend the most time with', so you have to ask yourself are you spending time with the right people to achieve your goals and aspirations in life or did some of these people help propel you to the ocean floor. If the answer is the latter then move on, you can always make new friends and your life will be better for it. You can visualize this as the ocean equivalent of having a keep-net, albeit an emotional one, into which you are going to look and examine the species you find there, if they are not what you want close to you open your net and release them back into the ocean of life, they will swim off and find their own path.

Now having done some personal development and having assessed your emotional keep-net you have begun a process of transformation. In your life so far, you have been conditioned and taught to be the ocean equivalent of white-bait, which explains your current feelings. You have always been told that your opinions do not count, and that one person cannot change the world, and depending on your social class you may have been conditioned on what and how much you can achieve in life. That is because we live in a society which is the ocean equivalent of a fish farm. Government, be it world or local would be the ocean equivalent of the fishermen and have a vested interested in the fish farm, ensuring it is well cared for and maintained, but undisturbed. Once you understand that you live in a fish farm, you can of course still choose to live there, but where has that gotten you in your life? I am going to suggest that you need to become something different in the ocean of life, an octopus. The octopus has qualities you are going to need in your recovery, it is highly intelligent, can rapidly learn new behaviour and use tools and of course it can get away quickly when it spots trouble.

Now you face a critical choice in your journey through the ocean of life, you can adopt your new view of life and let personal development and the rest of the octopus code begin to transform you. You can then swim off into the ocean of life and explore what it has to offer free from the influence of the fish farm. The alternative is to remain a fish and carry on with your old life and just muddle through, but you have to accept if you do this there is a greater chance you may end up back on the ocean floor of life or stuck in the fish farm.

In summary, in this chapter, I have covered how to deal with negative people who will be the ocean equivalent of jellyfish in your life, through personal development which you can use to begin to transform yourself and grow in self-confidence, and how you can view personal development like the ocean equivalent of a leather-back turtle which eats jellyfish. This will then allow you to transform yourself from the small fish you have been all your ocean life, once you choose to become an octopus, you are then ready for the next step in the Octopus code.

CHAPTER 3 - MAPPING THE 'OCEAN OF LIFE'

Exploring the ocean of life is quite a scary concept for many people and it will take you a while to become a fully-fledged octopus, you will probably start off being an octo-fish, half fish half octopus, while you experiment with the concept of being free from the fish farm, which is perfectly fine. The following affirmation will help 'I am swimming in the ocean of life, as an octopus free from all burdens in life, and ready to reach new heights I never thought were possible for me'. However, before you swim off into the ocean of life you need to map and understand its layers clearly, swim off without doing this and you will end up easy prey for the sharks and other hazards which lurk in the ocean of life. Imagine you were planning a long voyage on the real ocean, would you set off with no map or means of navigation and hope to reach your destination? Of course, you wouldn't, but this is what many people do in life, just hoping things will all work out and somehow, they will achieve their life goals.

Therefore, the third step of the Octopus code is to map the ocean of life. However, before you begin to map the ocean of life it is important to differentiate between hopes, dreams and life goals. A hope is something you hope will happen, but you have no idea how to make it happen. A dream is simply a goal with no date or deadline, but a life goal is something you want to achieve in your life, which you have a plan to achieve, and can set a deadline by which you want to achieve it. In order to progress, you need to transform as many of your unfulfilled hopes and dreams into life goals as you can. You need to do this because, quite simply, unfulfilled hopes and dreams are the ocean equivalent of anchors and chains. These will tether you to the ocean floor of life, sometimes if the anchor is really stuck the only thing you can do is cut the line and move on if you don't want them to prevent you from rising up the ocean of life. However, life goals are the ocean of life equivalent of mussels, the favourite food of the Octopus. This food will fill you with passion and will supercharge you in your journey upwards in the ocean of life. It is also important to remember that it is almost certain that you won't be able to transform all your dreams and hopes, into life goals at this particular stage in your life, that's okay just focus on the ones that mean the most to you at the present time. Of course, as your life changes you may be able to transform more into life goals, maybe even some you thought were previously impossible.

You are now ready to understand the layers of the ocean of life, establish a clear map of it in your head. You will then know how far up it you need to rise to achieve what you want in life.

The ocean of life resembles the real ocean in that it also contains four main layers, which I will now describe.

The first main layer in ocean of life is the Abyss Layer. As in the actual ocean one of the characteristics of this layer is that everything here lives under extreme pressure. Because of it's position as the bottom layer, it is low in food and completely dark. These facts make it hard to survive here and meet a partner. This is the layer in the ocean of life a lot of people are born into, I am sure you recognise a high-pressure environment, where survival is difficult. At this level in the ocean of life the darkness represents a lack of spiritual awareness, quite a lot of people at this level are literally 'sleepwalking' through their lives, they get up, go to work, come home watch TV, go to bed and repeat for 40 years. There is nothing wrong with that some people are happy doing that, I would classify them as the tripod fish in the ocean of life, because they have three firm anchors to their ocean floor baseline which help them to survive at this level. However, these anchors can also hold them at a fixed level without a change in thinking.

There are also the other personality types at this level, that I have already mentioned, jellyfish, sharks, whales, anglerfish and starfish.

Of course, at this level in the ocean it is possible to achieve some life goals, at this point it is good to think again about what your life goals truly are, what do you need in your life to be truly happy? If you feel unfulfilled and find yourself wanting more in life, then you need move up to next layer in the ocean of life, and this is going to take time if you want to do it successfully. In the same way that a deep-sea diver has to return to the surface in stages to avoid decompression sickness, you need to give yourself time to acclimatise to a new layer in the ocean of life. Many times, in life we have seen someone experience a meteoric rise to fame, be unable to handle it and lose everything, mostly this is because they have had insufficient time to acclimatise to being in a different layer of the ocean of life. You could look on each of your goals in life as having a decompression time, which corresponds to how far up the ocean of life you have to go to achieve them, depending on your goals some will obviously take longer to achieve than others. Clearly if some of your life goals are spiritual you are going to find them very difficult to achieve in the spiritual darkness of the Abyss layer and you will need to move up the ocean of life.

The next layer in the ocean of life is the Midnight zone. The Midnight zone is different from the Abyss layer in that it is not a layer in complete darkness, there is some light. However, this light only comes from the people in this zone who are just taking the first step towards spiritual awareness. Within this zone there is also the 'false' light which comes from people with anglerfish personalities who also operate in this zone as well as the abyss, you need to be aware of this and not be drawn in by the latest shining light which claims to transform your life. If you reach this zone you will have formulated some clear life goals and you need to stick to them if you want to be successful in this zone. Luckily there will be some people in the Midnight layer who like yourself are taking their initial steps on their path to achieving their life goals and some of them will be happy to help you. Not all of these

17

people will have octopus' personalities of course, some people who would be blobfish in the ocean of life operate at this level. These people have enough energy to escape from the fish farm and flourish at this level but if they move up to a higher level in the ocean of life, they may be unable to physically or mentally operate at this new level, unless they are willing to change personality. This is another reason why some people cannot handle new found fame and fortune which moves them higher up the ocean of life. There is of course a key difference between the ocean of life and the real ocean, in the real ocean a shark is born a shark and cannot change. In the ocean of life, we all have the capacity to become what we wish through change, of course some people, for whatever reason, do not want to change. Therefore sometimes, you have to respect that and move on, if you want a smooth passage upward in the ocean of life.

Another personality type you will encounter in the Midnight zone are people who would be electric eels in the ocean of life. These types of people you will trust initially, but that is their game plan, then from nowhere they will literally stun you by saying, or doing, something unexpected to you which is hurtful. This sort of attack can be quite crippling as these types of people may appear to be well informed, and thus difficult to ignore. Remember just ask yourself, have they ever lived your life? Do they truly know your situation? The only person who truly knows what you are capable of is you, and also remember no electric eel ever ate an octopus!

A helpful personality type in the Midnight layer are people who are just embracing spirituality but are on a different path to you. These people would be lantern fish in the ocean of life. They resemble lantern fish in that they are small and are not in direct competition for food with the octopus but emit a guiding light which can be followed, also lantern fish are capable of swimming to the surface of the ocean of life, so by following them they can take you a long way on your journey upward. Clearly people with lantern fish personalities are a valuable guide on your journey upwards, as you can be sure they will guide you safely without trying to eat you! They are a stark contrast to people at this level who resemble luminous sharks, they can also lead you to the surface but will have no qualms about eating you, should the need or opportunity arise.

It is also important to remember that the lack of spiritual light at this level, means that no spiritual food can grow at this level, which would be the real ocean equivalent of phytoplankton. This lack of spiritual phytoplankton means that everyone at this level are potentially either predators or scavengers. This means you are very vulnerable whilst you are at this level, and you need to be aware of this. However, if your life goals don't require much spiritual development, the small amount of guiding light here, which comes from others, may be enough to inspire you and the Midnight Zone may be as far up the ocean of life as you need to go.

The next layer in the ocean of life is the Twilight Zone, in this layer there is now enough spiritual light for spiritual phytoplankton to grow. There are many types of phytoplankton in this zone, which type you choose to eat can have a profound effect on your development and your path to your life goals. The different types of spiritual food means it is possible to have experiences in this zone which are not possible in the lower zones, because of the darkness and lack of food.

However, this zone also has its own hazards, it is important to remember the spiritual food in this zone is filtered by the types of people present in it, so it can be altered and may not be as pure as the spiritual food in the next layer of the ocean of life. The spiritual food available in this zone is also still limited in type and amount, which means everyone in this zone survives by either eating this food or is a potential predator.

There are some people in this zone who are the ocean of life equivalent of angel sharks, they look like angels but annoy or upset them, and they have the bite of a shark very capable of devouring you. There are also some people in this zone who are the ocean of life equivalent of swordfish, big fish with a sword capable of cutting you to ribbons at the slightest excuse. The final type of people you will encounter at this level are the ocean equivalent of clams, they will stay open for a while sometimes just to lure you into their shell, perhaps with promise of some pearls of wisdom, then without warning the shell slams shut. The person literally clams up and you may be trapped inside, or be shut off from them for a very long time before they open up again, indeed they may never do. The lesson here is not to be a pearl diver we can all be tempted by 'shiny object syndrome' but remember very few clams contain a pearl.

Of course, with octopus thinking, you are now better prepared to deal with these hazards, indeed they may be necessary to encounter for your personal development. Remember your personal development turtle will always protect you against these people. Thus, if your life goals demand a moderate amount of spiritual and personal development, then you need to aim for the Twilight zone of the ocean of life. Because in this zone there is just enough spiritual phytoplankton to allow for a partial spiritual and personal awakening, which is all you may need or indeed be comfortable with.

The final layer in the ocean of life is the Sunlight Zone. In this layer of the ocean of life, spiritual light is abundant and there is enough to support all who reside here. The abundance of light in this zone allows coral reefs to form, which in the ocean of life are the equivalent of knowledge bases, based on collected experience. These reefs are unique to this zone, they simply cannot survive in the lower zones as they depend on spiritual light to survive. In this zone these reefs provide an unparalleled array of knowledge, unavailable anywhere else. If these reefs are accessed correctly, and with due caution, there is enough information here to achieve most life goals. However, just like the other zones in the ocean of life, this zone and the reef are not without their hazards.

Among the reefs there are people who, in the ocean of life are anemones, they cling to the corals of knowledge, perhaps in the mistaken belief they are somehow protecting it. They may sting unsuspecting people who are the tiny fish of life with their poison venom, sending them back to the ocean floor and scaring more people away. Thus, perpetuating the myth that not everyone can access the reef safely, and that there is dangerous knowledge in there. There is also within the reefs of knowledge people who are clown fish in the ocean of life. These people, through years of association with anemones, have become immune to their sting and are thus able to swim through the reefs of knowledge freely accumulating a great deal of the knowledge along the way. They are thus very useful to know and may be able to help you greatly on your journey. However it also important to remember that they rely on anemones for their protection and will have accumulated some of their poison by association, so if they are attacked, or feel threatened, they will be a problem to deal with. Thus, it is necessary to exercise a great deal of caution when dealing with this type of person.

If you reach this level in the ocean of life, you should be a big enough octopus to be impervious to the sting of anemone, but if sting of the anemone comes as a shock to you, don't let it send you back crashing to the ocean floor, remember it is merely a sign. The sign that the sting is giving you, is that you need a new guide in your personal development. Fortunately, at this level there is an abundance of sea turtles, so simply let your old turtle buddy swim away and pick a new and different turtle as your new personal development ally, who is more suitable to help at this stage of your life development.

At this level you will also encounter people who are dolphins in the ocean of life, these playful people are smart, friendly but also very hedonistic, which is great if that is what you want in your life, but not so good if you want to achieve something more practical, so you need to consider how many people with dolphin type personalities you allow into your life.

Also present in the sunlight zone are people who are cleaner wrasse in the ocean of life. These people may be therapists of many kinds who can help clear unhelpful behaviours or attachments, or they can even be service orientated people who gain joy by putting others on the path to their life goals. They can be approached safely and are generally helpful on the journey to achieving life goals.

Another useful type of person found in this zone are people who are angelfish in the ocean of life. These people are literally angelic in nature and would do anything to help anybody. They are also very protective once you get to know them, and they will protect you from your harshest critics, remember angelfish eat jellyfish.

There is a vast amount of spiritual information available in the Sunlight zone, though some of it is closely guarded, there is also a great deal of help and certain types of people in this zone who cannot exist in the other zones of the ocean of life. Therefore, are your life goals more ambitious? Do they require a large amount of personal or spiritual development? Then you have to reach this zone.

In summary, in this chapter, I have explained the need to distinguish between hopes, dreams and life goals. I also described the four layers in the ocean of life, so that you can now understand their characteristics, some of the people present at each of these levels, and the experiences available there. Armed with this knowledge you can evaluate your life goals and have a clear idea of how far up the ocean of life you need to go to achieve them. This will give you a reasonable chance of achieving these goals in a realistic time scale, providing you do not fall prey to some of the pitfalls of the ocean of life, which are discussed in the next step of the Octopus code in Chapter 4.

CHAPTER 4 - AVOIDING THE PITFALLS IN THE OCEAN OF LIFE

In the previous chapter I discussed the importance of mapping the ocean of life and having a clear map in your head of where you need to be to achieve your life goals. This is important because without such a map you will get discouraged, disillusioned and impatient in achieving them, all major factors which can ultimately prevent you from reaching them. Clearly this is one pitfall in the ocean of life. There are of course several other pitfalls in the ocean of life which can prevent you from attaining your life goals. Therefore step 4 in the Octopus code is **avoid the pitfalls in the ocean of life**.

Let's take a look at some of the other pitfalls in the ocean of life, the most obvious is passivity which is the ocean of life equivalent of algae. This alga grows when you continue to do nothing and take no action, you can read all the self-help books there are, including this one, but if you take no action of course nothing will happen. There are also a lot of creatures in the ocean of life who feed off this type of alga and have a vested interest in stopping you from taking action. People who have jellyfish personalities being one example. This algae has a different composition to the spiritual phytoplankton of the Twilight zone and if after a while you become encrusted in it you will find it difficult to move. This is why many people find change difficult, but remember our old friend the turtle of personal development is the solution, as turtles love to eat algae. Also, if you get to the sunlight zone in the ocean of life there are people in this zone who are the ocean of life equivalent of cleaner wrasse that can help clear some of the algae of passivity from you and help you on the path to achieving your life goals.

Another pitfall in the ocean of life is the fear of taking action, which you can allow to become sea monsters that terrify you and hold you back, so you become imprisoned by that fear. This is another reason people fail to achieve their life goals. There was a time when people believed there really were sea monsters at the end of the world which ate boats and sailors who tried to sail around the world, so no-one dared to try to do this. Then of course Francis Drake and his expedition did it and proved there were no sea monsters just undiscovered lands. If you want to achieve your life goals you need to throw off some of your fears and have an explorer mentality just like Drake and his expedition. Think what could you achieve if you became bolder and became an explorer of ocean of life like the octopus. You have already acquired a lot more knowledge and life experience than many of the simple fish of the ocean of life and that will protect you from a lot of your fears and you will realise they are unfounded. If you want movement in your life and to move up the ocean of life just like in the real ocean you have to start to swim. Remember we're are only born with 2 fears the fear of falling and the fear of loud noises. All your other fears have been learned from the ocean of life during your development in it to where you are now. A quote from Will Smith is relevant here 'Danger is real but fear is a choice'.

You may mistakenly believe fear protects you but it does not, fear is a negative emotion, a monster can never protect you. I believe love is a far better protector. If you love yourself so much that you want to do something to help yourself, you are far more likely to take action.

The last two pitfalls in the ocean of life are the equivalent of depth charges and minefields.

Depth charges in the ocean of life are normally released by

people at a higher level who have a vested interest in preventing you from reaching their level and your full potential. At a certain point you will come onto their radar and they will perceive you as a threat and begin to attack you. The attack will be intended to hurt and discourage you and it may be difficult to take emotionally and mentally. A good strategy to overcome this pitfall is to employ a tactic of real submarines which is simply to exhaust the attacker. Remember that they only have a limited supply of depth charges, once they see their attacks are having no effect, they will have no option but to give up and pursue someone else. It is also wise to remember the closer a depth charge gets the more damage it does, indeed it relies on getting close to be an effective weapon. Thus, if you are able to keep your attacker distant from yourself and not absorb the charge, you will render their weapon useless and be able to move through the ocean of life untroubled. Of course, it is also important not to self-sabotage during such an attack, otherwise you can magnify it's effect. Once again, the turtle of personal development can come to your rescue, use it to distance yourself from the attacks until they cease.

Minefields manifest themselves in the ocean of life as a seemingly insurmountable set of problems. How often have you said to yourself "That would be a minefield to sort with all the problems that would involve!". When confronted with a minefield in the ocean of life you have three options, you can let the fear of it terrify you and remain stagnant and stuck in your life, as I discussed previously using the sea monster analogy. You could also take a detour in your life and avoid it, but that may mean moving a long way from your life goals and literally taking your life off track. The third option is to find someone who can be a mentor to you and be the ocean of life equivalent of a minesweeper going before you and helping you effortlessly clear them and move upward in the ocean of life. Of course, if you choose this option you need to be certain that your chosen mentor has the skill and experience to neutralise the mines as you pass through the field. Picking the wrong mentor who is not suitable for the task can result in serious problems and can even be a surefire route back to the floor of the ocean of life. Trust your intuition in picking a mentor, it should be someone who is in tune with your values and ideals and has already travelled through a few minefields in the ocean of life. You need someone who has achieved some of the goals you aspire to, it's wise to remember a quote from Marian Wright Edelman 'You can't be what you can't see'.

In this chapter I have discussed how to overcome the pitfalls in the ocean of life. These pitfalls are often the reason people fail to progress in the ocean of life and complain that they are 'stuck' in their life. Equipped with the knowledge enabling you to over-come these pitfalls, you can move on in your life and are ready for the next step of the Octopus code, which I will discuss in Chapter 5.

CHAPTER 5 - JETTISON THE POLLUTANTS OF THE PAST

Now you are aware of the pitfalls of the ocean, the next step in the Octopus code is to **jettison the pollutants of the past.** There are five main emotional pollutants which you may be hanging on to from the past, these are envy, jealousy, anger, guilt and lack of self-worth. These pollutants can be visualized as the ocean of life equivalent of pirates, who hold you captive and rob you of your treasure. Think about it for a moment, has feeling any of these emotions ever truly served you well? Feeling these emotions can never reverse what has happened in the past, you cannot rewrite history, but you can alter how you react to your history. We all have a habit of coming to rest on the shipwrecks in the ocean of life, these being the mistakes of our past. If we are not careful, we can become resident on these shipwrecks, unable to move on enslaved by the pirate pollutants, which thrive there. This is, of course, another reason why people fail to progress to the level they wish in the ocean of life. Think about it, how many times have you said "How can I, in my situation with all my problems, do this?". That is what I call 'shipwreck' thinking. If you are suffering from 'shipwreck' thinking, then you will find it difficult to achieve what you want in life. Some might say that an easy way to short circuit 'shipwreck' thinking is to win the lottery or acquire a large amount of money in some other way. This is the ocean of life equivalent of getting into a submarine fuelled by money, it will indeed rescue you from a shipwreck and the power of its ballast tanks will blow away your emotional pollutants for a time. However, as I explained in chapter 1, money is a finite resource which will run out, so you have learn how to pilot your submarine and understand how to refuel it, if you take this route out of trouble. If you don't it will eventually fill with the emotional pollutants of the past and you may sink back down to the shipwreck or sometimes even to the ocean floor of life, and be left with nothing again. This is another reason why lottery winners sometimes end up losing all their money and being unhappy again.

The best way to overcome 'shipwreck' thinking is firstly to forgive yourself for the mistakes of the past, you possibly did not mean to do everything you did, but you acted with the best information that you had at the time. Forgiveness is a very powerful thing, just try sitting down and forgiving yourself for every mistake that you have ever made in your life. The next thing is to confront each of the pirate pollutants, envy, jealousy, anger, guilt and lack of self-worth. When you are feeling these emotions, try to understand what causes you to feel each of them, and really understand how you came to feel that way, it is important to get at the underlying cause of each of these pollutants and then let each of these pollutants go. Use the affirmation 'I am on my way up the ocean of life, the residual pollutants of envy, jealousy, anger, guilt and lack of self-worth no longer serve me, I let them leave me and I travel lighter upon my journey'. Then visualise confronting each pirate pollutant and letting them go. Being part of a pirate crew sucks, tell your pirate pollutants you quit and you are moving on, jettison them and you will feel much better and be prepared to move on up in the ocean of life and achieve your goals. You can imagine the pirate pollutants returning to the shipwreck and being locked away in separate cabins, so you can move on in your life.

Some people may say that envy, jealousy, anger, guilt and lack of self-worth are emotions which can motivate you to achieve goals in life, and this is true to a certain extent. The question you have to ask yourself is, if you are relying on these emotions to motivate you, are you trying to achieve your life goals for the right reasons or are they even what you truly want from life? Perhaps they have even been imposed on you by someone else. Remember these emotions are pollutants and used enough they will eventually pollute your life, which is why no matter how much success some people have in their lives it is not enough, because they are motivated by some, or all, of these pollutant emotions. Taking our pirate analogy to its logical conclusion, most pirates will serve the captain while it suits them but eventually, they will turn on him and he will end up walking the plank into the ocean, not a desirable outcome for any life. Another way to view it is that pollutant emotions only allow you to become a soldier in the ocean of the life. A soldier will only fight for pay, in this case the payoff from dispelling these emotions for a while, but what happens when there is no more pay, then a soldier will give up the fight. This is why people sometimes don't achieve their life goals. Also, if times get difficult a soldier may dessert abruptly and disappear down the ocean again. However, if you truly jettison your pollutant emotions you become a warrior in the ocean of life, a warrior fights because they believe in themself and the quest they are on, and does not give up until they complete that quest. You have to decide if you prefer to be an ocean warrior, like the octopus, or to remain a mere soldier fish subject to the orders of whoever or whatever emotions control you at any particular time in your life. I would suggest it is better to be an ocean warrior than a soldier, if you agree then you are ready for the next step in the Octopus code, which I will discuss in Chapter 6.

CHAPTER 6 - AVOID BECOMING A MUTANT OCTOPUS

Now that you have jettisoned the toxic pollutants of the past, you are ready for the next step in the Octopus code, which is to **avoid becoming a mutant octopus**. If you allow this to happen, it will have a severe negative impact on your ability to achieve your life goals. There are three types of mutation which can affect your ability to be an octopus in the ocean of life. Firstly, some people can become what I call a toxic octopus, what happens here is the person gets excited about self-help and spiritual development and takes some action, but then when they realise that it takes effort and it can be hard, they give up. This person will then, probably unknowingly, self-sabotage their own life and also sabotage other people's lives, by telling them self-help and spiritual development is rubbish and doesn't work. This can be a problem, as people on their journey up from the ocean floor of life will be influenced by these types of people, as they may look on them as authority figures or someone whose opinion they can trust. If people are telling you self-help and spiritual development is a waste of time, you have to consider whether you can trust the opinion of the person telling you this. Do they have a reason for this? Perhaps they have had some bad experiences in their life, which have stunted the amount of self-help or spiritual development they were able to do, or maybe they tried to move up to a level in the ocean of life they were not ready for yet. You have to consider this when people try to give you advice about achieving your life goals. If you are getting advice from someone who is a toxic octopus the chances are, you may become one yourself. Luckily, if you find yourself becoming a toxic octopus, it is not terminal and indeed there is a simple solution, you just have to recognise that you are holding yourself back and are guilty of self-sabotage. Occasional self-sabotage is okay, everyone including myself is guilty of the odd self-deprecating remark, self-doubt and fear of the unknown, which I talked about in previous chapters. However, long term continual self-sabotage is not good for anyone. In a similar process to the one I discussed in the last chapter, you have to look at why you are self-sabotaging, there may be more than one reason and it could be that the reason is due to external forces. You can also be self-sabotaging just out of defiance and spite, because someone told you to do something who you don't necessarily like or perceive as an authority figure, so you do the opposite of what they told you. This is sometimes the case, even if you know deep down that their advice is correct.

 In either case think, do these forces internal or external have my best interests at heart or are they the ocean of life equivalent of micro plastics, ubiquitous but insidious and capable of poisoning everything in the ocean? If you are being poisoned by these micro plastics, then a good visualisation is to see a dark octopus spitting out little black balls, until you become a bright white octopus and are once again an octopus of the light. While you do this visualisation say to yourself, ' I give up all self-sabotage and reject any emotions or forces, internal or external, which promote it. I am a confident, powerful, unstoppable octopus on my way up through the ocean of life. On my journey I get to deservedly achieve my life goals.'

The second type of mutant octopus is the octo-parrot. This is simply someone who has read many books on self-help and self-development but has taken no action. This can be a fundamental problem, if you are going to have any success in life, you have to change what you have done previously. Clearly what you have done in the past has not worked for you or you wouldn't be in this position in your life. If you want your life to change you need to take action, otherwise you will simply remain an octo-parrot, someone who went some of the way, is no a longer fish but not an octopus, just someone who knows all the principles and the action to take, but never did anything. Does that sound like a good place to be in your life to you? A quote from Jim Rohn is appropriate here 'Discipline weighs ounces, regret weighs tons'. Don't be burdened by regret if you recognise you are an octo-parrot, it is never too late to take action you can still achieve those life goals you just have to start moving those octopus' tentacles. In order to move those octopus' tentacles, you have to consider what is holding you back, I have mentioned some possible obstacles in previous chapters. The most common obstacle is people of various types in your life who can hold you back, a good visualisation to remove these people and allow yourself to progress is called the 'speargun visualisation'. In this visualisation you imagine a fine strong silver wire being tied around the obstacle, and the long length of the rest of the wire is attached to a spear, which is placed in a speargun. The gun is then fired so the spear goes to the ocean floor anchoring the obstacle at its current level so you can move on. There is course always the danger, that the obstacle can break free and come after you. But if you are truly determined nothing can stop you. A quotation from Richard Dawkins is important to remember here 'The rabbit runs quicker than the fox because the rabbit is running for his life, but the fox is only running for his dinner.' If you keep moving onward and upward eventually your pursuer will give up, even if they have a shark personality, because they are always looking for the 'easy' meal, don't be that meal.

The final type of mutant octopus is the giraffeopus. This is someone who has become so obsessed with the spiritual side of their life that they can become disconnected with reality, they may also be guilty of 'shiny object' syndrome. This type of person is always seeking answers in spirituality from books, religion, or the internet, hoping that there is some great answer or some big secret which will put their life straight and allow them to achieve their life goals. Again, people of this type can fall prey to the sharks in the ocean of life who are happy to peddle this belief to them and of course make a good living from it. Remember sharks follow their food source, once they perceive you are no longer food they will give up and move onto an easier meal. Don't give in to the sharks. Sometimes as an octopus you have to learn to spray your ink, and in the confusion, make a quick getaway as in the end it will be for the best. Once you have made your escape and you realise you have mutated in to a giraffeopus, firstly you have to take yourself calmly to one side and really ask yourself what you are trying to achieve in your life, and how important it is to you. Then you have to ask yourself, are you going about it in the right way and getting the best help and support? There is of course some help and support in this and other books, on the internet, and in religion but I don't believe that any of these things have all the answers to achieving life goals, because all goals begin with action. A quote from Vince Lombardi is very relevant here 'The only time success comes before work is in the dictionary'. Ask yourself are you taking the right actions to achieve your life goals if the answer is no, then you need to put yourself back on track. In order to put yourself back on the right track, imagine your giraffe head shrinking and that you are returning to a regular focused octopus' shape. Use the affirmation 'I am grateful for all I have in my life and I am ready to swim in the ocean of life again, taking action and seeking new self-led adventures'. If you have found the track difficult in the past, a quote by Zig Ziglar may be helpful 'Difficult roads often lead to beautiful destinations'.

In this chapter I have discussed three types of octopus mutation, which although different, all lead to the same outcome of inaction, which is why many people fail to achieve their life goals. So the lesson here is don't let yourself mutate. As a non-mutated octopus you are now ready for the next step of the Octopus code, which I will discuss in Chapter 7.

CHAPTER 7 - FACING THE PORPOISE OF PROCRASTINATION

The next step of the Octopus code is to face the porpoise of procrastination, this is a very powerful creature in the ocean of life and is one which has stifled or snuffed out many life goals. The porpoise of procrastination is a very beguiling creature, and I would almost liken it to the mythical 'sirens' which were said to lure sailors onto rocks in Greek mythology. Fortunately, the rocks it traps you on are only emotional, and it is possible to escape from these rocks if you wish to. The porpoise of procrastination is also a very friendly creature who seems harmless at first, but looks can be deceptive. In order to examine the effect this creature can have on your life, ask yourself how many games of 'Candy Crush' or 'Angry Birds' have you played to avoid a difficult situation in your life, which although stressful, if you face it could be life changing. That's the porpoise of procrastination beginning to take hold of you. How many times have you said "I will start my diet next week" or "I will start a new business once I have a particular item", which in most cases is not vital, again this allows porpoise of procrastination to do his work and stop you from achieving your life goals.

The first step in overcoming the porpoise of procrastination is to recognise that you are a victim of this creature. There has to be a bit of self-assessment here, if you are briefly putting off an important task for a short period then that is okay, but if you put things off indefinitely or continually switch focus to avoid doing things, then you almost certainly have a problem. The next step is an important one, you need to ask yourself why you are procrastinating so much, particularly if the problem has become chronic and debilitating to the point where you are trapped on the emotional rocks. As I discussed in Chapter 1, you have to stop behaving like a limpet and acknowledge the mistakes of your past and move on, with effort you can free yourself from the emotional rocks. It is then possible to defeat the porpoise of procrastination with your new octopus thinking, which I am now going to explain further.

Before I talk about octopus thinking to overcome the porpoise of procrastination, it is important to mention that chronic procrastination can be a symptom of serious mental issues, such as ADHD, OCD, eating disorders, or depression so if you suspect you have any of these you should consult a health professional first. Once you have discounted these possibilities, you can begin to use octopus thinking.

The first principle of octopus thinking is that an octopus doesn't eat vegetables and hates broccoli, so everyday do your 'octopus broccoli' task first, that is something which is high priority, but you hate doing. That way it gets done, and you can then move on to lower priority tasks you enjoy doing.

The second principle of octopus thinking is when an octopus feeds, it uses its beak to break its prey into small chunks and then envelopes it. Can you find your octopus beak for a task, an insight which enables you to break it down into more bite-size pieces, and really devour it with relish? The third principle of octopus thinking is that an octopus always scans the ocean assessing the terrain and working out if it can fit into rocky crevices if it can't it moves on. In the same way, you need to assess if you can do the task in your current environment, can you fit in everything you want to? If not, you need to change your environment and let go of some things from the past. Perhaps you may have to examine your emotional keep-net, as you did in Chapter 2, and let some stuff, or people, out of it. When you examine your emotional keep-net you may find it now contains invasive species, the ocean of life equivalent of lionfish, which have forced their way into your life, but don't belong there. This can happen over time and you may need to clear them out in order to overcome procrastinating.

The last principle of octopus thinking is when an octopus faces attack from a predator, such as a shark on the ocean floor, it quickly builds a cover of shells where it can hide until the attacker has gone. This demonstrates the octopus understands that done is better than perfect. If the octopus tried to build a perfect shelter, then he would be eaten by the shark. If the cover isn't perfect and the shark gets in eventually, the octopus knows he can spray a jet of ink and most likely get away in the confusion. Thus, in the same way you need to recognise that 'done is better than perfect', if a task is not done right there is often a way to modify it, or alter it, so it has the desired outcome. The ability to do every task in your life perfectly, is very difficult to aspire to, and not possible for the vast majority of people. Thus, they don't do it for fear of not being perfect at it first time, and so it never gets done and the porpoise of procrastination wins. However, if you follow the four principles of octopus thinking that I have outlined you have the chance to defeat the porpoise of procrastination and move on in the quest to achieve your life goals. In the next chapter I will describe the final step of the Octopus code, that you will need in your journey through the ocean of life.

CHAPTER 8 - LEARNING TO SWIM AGAINST THE OCEAN TIDE

The final step of the Octopus code involves permanent movement, I have already spoken about taking small steps in previous chapters, but for change to become permanent, you have to take larger steps. This requires motivation, a lot of people lack motivation, but I think one of the biggest motivations is death. Death is the trawler man in the ocean of life, every day he casts out his nets, if you are unlucky you get caught, but every day you don't is a blessing. A quote from Les Brown is relevant here 'The graveyard is the richest place on earth' because here you will find all the life goals that were never fulfilled. But where there is life there is hope. That is a good start, ask yourself "what is the worst thing that could happen if I do a certain action on the path to my life goals?" There is a psychological technique known as 'fear rehearsing', which can help. This technique involves slowly dosing yourself with elements of your worst-case scenario, so that you realise you could survive it and you become desensitized to it. This technique is explained in the book 'Letters from a Stoic', by the great philosopher Seneca, who says if you have a fear of losing money 'Set aside a certain number of days, during which you shall be content with the scantiest and cheapest fare, with coarse and rough dress, saying to yourself all the while: **Is this the condition that I so feared?** '. Therefore, you can see, having survived your worst fears, your survival is not dependent on money, and you could take some steps on your path to your life goals without harm.

In the higher regions of the ocean of life there is also the problem of ghost nets, which are the real life equivalent of glass ceilings. These discarded nets act as invisible barriers and can be put there by people who have a vested interest in keeping you at the lower levels of the ocean of life, or they can be self-imposed. These nets trap you, using trauma from the past, and can send you back to the ocean floor of life or lead to you becoming a mutant octopus, as I discussed in chapter 6. This is also why, if you want permanent irreversible movement off the floor of the ocean of life, it is important to jettison the pollutants of the past as I discussed in chapter 5. Otherwise you will get so far off the ocean of life floor, but then these pollutants can cause you to veer off course and to become ensnared in the ghost nets. This is where the octopus thinking, I discussed in the last chapter helps, if you become trapped in a ghost net look for your octopus beak; an insight or experience from your past which can help you break free. Remember a sharp beak can easily cut through a net, but stay a fish and you will remain trapped.

Once you have the motivation, and can avoid the ghosts nets, you are now ready to permanently leave the floor of the ocean of life. Now another problem manifests itself as you get further away from the fish farm you have lived on; the tide will change and get strong, and very different to anything you have ever experienced. Do you have the courage to continue on that journey to reach your life goals? At this point it is important to remember if you are following the map of the ocean of life and you are lost, it is okay to stop and ask directions. It is important to ask directions from the right type of person, as there are people with all sorts of personalities in the ocean of life as I discussed in previous chapters. However, a lot of people never do this they just start off with the map, get lost, discard it and go back to ocean floor annoyed.

Ask yourself if you would do this on a real-life journey. Probably not, so why do it on your journey to achieve your life goals, and remember it is never too late to get help, pick up the map and start on the journey again.

 The last step in the Octopus code is sometimes you have to learn to swim against the tide of the ocean of life to achieve your life goals. It is true that conforming and swimming with the tide will get you so far, but it may take you to a destination that you don't want to go to. You may get lost when swimming against the tide, but you can always stop and ask for directions. You may also fall down on the way, but you need the courage to get back up and try again. A quote from Socrates is relevant here ' Falling down is not failure, failure comes when you stay where you have fallen'.

This is the difference between an octopus and a fish mentality in the ocean of life. A person with a fish mentality will just keep swimming, following the tide hoping it will all work out, and they will get to the right destination, but if the tide changes, they lack the ability to swim against it and are often sucked back down to the ocean floor of life. A person with an octopus mentality understands how the ocean of life is made up and can think how to get a particular point in it. They also have the strength and courage to propel themselves there even against the tide, and do not give up until they get there. At this point it is important to recall a quotation from Roy T. Bennett 'Great things don't come from comfort zones' and another from Rita Mae Brown ' Insanity is doing the same thing over and over again and expecting different results'. The final question you have to ask yourself, now you have all the steps in the Octopus code, is do I want to remain a fish in the ocean of life and allow a large collective of others to think for me? or do I want to be an octopus and swim freely in the ocean of life, thinking freely for myself, and become incredibly individualistic on the path to achieving my life goals? Now is your time to rise up from the depths of the ocean of life. Lastly I am reminded of a quote by Malcom Muggeridge 'Never forget that only dead fish swim with the stream'. This is also true in the ocean of life, what is the point is of always swimming with the tide even a dead fish can do that. Thank you for reading this book, and may it empower you to live a better life and achieve your life goals.

ABOUT THE AUTHOR

Royston Graham Lawrence

Originally a PhD Chemist with 10 years experience in academic research. In 2008 I switched fields and began working in Complementary therapies with a keen interest in energy work and self-help. This book is the culmination of all I have learned from working in this field, some-times literally when at festivals, for 12 years. I hope you enjoy it and may it empower you to reach your life goals. I currently work from my own practice under the business name 'Roy's Holistic Therapies'. I currently offer Indian Head massage, Reiki and Crystal Therapy. You are welcome to contact me through my website at https://www.holisticroy.co.uk

Printed in Great Britain
by Amazon